Laughter You See

Laughter You See

Nicholas Panagakos

To order additional copies of this book, contact:
Xlibris Corporation
1-888-795-4274
www.Xlibris.com
Orders@Xlibris.com
96880

Contents

About The Author

By Kelly M. McGuire

Nick Panagakos is the finger on the arrhythmic pulse of our generation. Never before has the depravity of post recession America been captured in such a sincere yet uncertain way. The true measure however is not the stylistic integrity, but the complete lack of pretension that has become a staple among hipster nations. The stories contained here have been lived by nearly every estranged 20 something in these waning days of Babylon. Anxiety is cherished, absurdity is disciplined and the cult of personality that has followed Nick around since a small town in Connecticut is all too visible.

This is the death of Gonzo journalism.

K.M.M.
9:24 P.M.
April 4, 2011

You can Often get out.

A Note on the Text

Sleep is left for weeks, which made of days left, of the nights where fire spits out youthful optimism checked above the door of possibilities that mount along cold riverbanks driving clear perception in times of desperation caused by cloudy nomenclature from specters out from stories with passionate experience gathered through active participation in the organized clockwork where fact and gratification co-mingle with abbreviation & exaggeration to create a whole of truth peppered with influences leering all the while as chariots spin to twirl invisible dancers that hold nothing more than what they need to complete their predetermined task of weaving targets along with absurdities that nip and pull the modern mind with no regard to health or comfort sought by that miniscule commander who claims to be the one in control of destinations which began not of their own decisive will but by sadistic gestures of bullying pitch pipes through assorted valleys where life has always sprung to keep the order of animals keen to suggestive poses that, more often than not, could prevent explosive ambitions from leaving marked trails that point to lineage, expectations, success, fashion, or other topical hobbies of septic cause and effect.

Early Bird Note
For Leonard Cohen

"Blasted as ever,
wrapping homespun weave,
drinking whole glass thoughts,
through quiet felonies."

This smell fresh paint pierces,
counting clueless correspondence clearly,
all of which is helplessly routine.

Caught in closed door mentality,
(and break neck) speed,
social engagements falter.

Necessary rest brought through
barbarism rhythms chain
smoking signal signs and
lemon aide push poison.

"A great mistake was this
polite attempt in and of conversation.
'I never said that I was brave'." L.C.

Blasting Caps & Lightning

Songs that pass in movements break
            and bend
the open solitude.

When sterile cuts from post production
            march on
evenings cool and dry.

Thoughts of recreational deviance
            smile through
that vacant stair.

And all the while reminiscence blows
            like hot
beer from tailpipes.

Fools would have you thought about
            or in
deliciously antiquated vibrations.

Recounting hesitated missions if
            draped as
curtains as directed.

Stroll on these abandoned plans
            like most
lovers who waste kisses.

            The lingered action/passing time.

Goals that spread the sheets
            and floor
can hold a brief attention span.

Apologetic genealogy crippled this
            on point
reasoning as philanthropy.

Flames of scented bees like all
            good things
bloated quick and free.

iclappedihandsilaughediyou
rumble tumble through glass.

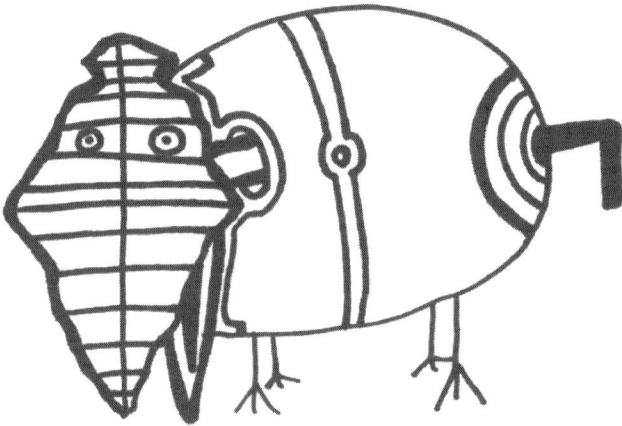

A Sinner's Grocery List

Never keep guests.
Don't create anything.
Assume to settle for convenience over love.
Drive the bitter bus.
Make hideous faces.
Curse.
Don't do a don't.
Do do a do.
Contemplate human sacrifice.
Drink.
Smoke.
Blow.
Suck.
Kiss.
Fuck.
Drive.
Ride.
Eat.
Run.
Play.
Fold.
Swim.
Nail.
Make.
Wipe.
Smile.
Burn.
Zip.
Wash.
Sleep.

Blood Milk Bible Salesmen

Those blood milk bible salesmen go peddlin' on
            cross eyed saunters.
They venture in gauging jaunts with
            no shoes or coats.
Police watch idly bystanders with homeless
            vocabularies press their intentions
                    against destinations that smell familiar.
Some kitten curls in diapers made by
            designer perverts;
            and those dogs will whine in line
                    for the scraps of treachery.

Who, Me?
            The ever vigilant loaf?

I delve in discotheques laced with vinegar
            to attempt a drastic change
                    in the weather.

                            Nothing seems to suit this.

The hours of progressive access
            can't keep up with plans formulated
                    as soon as they fail.

As soon as soon
            Too soon too soon
                    Be gone be gone
And kiss goodnight.

Until the moon sinks to sea
     and all those patent leather constructs
          tip-toe shuffle off and in with the
               hand bags of their sister crocodile.
I sink to rise and fall in awkward polychromatic
     spins that weave rain and winds to guide me.
With no set direction I sidestep the cobras
     and press on your arm.
          Without even trying,
           I push you away.

Dotting the Cross

Living experience replaying,
rebuking,
revolting consultant's intuitive time.
Believing a positive preference
unfolding the action bestowed
with a wandering eye.
Blowing a kiss of the number one fan
to the glowing electric empirical boss.
Chalk it around the inside of the line
but remember to count it as dotting the cross.
Coloring copperhead landscapes politely
with sails in my hair and a handle of wine.
Touch my inside of the shuttle discretely
to feed me a morsel and hand me a line.
Speaking with accents of no man's land worthless
we fuel aggravations while wasting no time.
Highways and byways in separate fashion
dislocating lemons that suck on old limes.
Black and blue badges mark officers timely
we're all in a hurry with no room to spare.
Burning the yearning of churning discerning
displays of a monster who tried not to care.

Sober & Honest

Dampened turbines hum in steady song
    lighting lamps *with lethargic
enthusiasm.
Peddling up brick walkways and
    calculating time & distance to
your door.
Crawling through windows on
    iced lacquer ledges and breathing steady
as she goes.
Invited—
    —but unexpected.
Startled—
    —but glad.
                Sober & Honest—
—a lying Drunk.

Those kisses, particular,
    sweet water off the vine.
        And part great fruits of
            poisoned brackish gullies.
                Behind those trembling doors
                we awoke to bombardment.
              Allow me the pleasure
            of an explanation.

                                    *or without

Etiquette

We've left your problems
bleated dry and calm
upon bone marrow meals
distributed thusly.
Combining theory and luck
with circumstances.
There won't be permission
or forgiveness
for the potential
or the fuss.
So leave your work
and commit to run
in corridors lined
with cotton.
And never be compelled
for apologetic books
on the etiquette of genocide.

Deep in
the heart
of Texas.

Bauble

Should bauble stray and wayfarer doom
perspective looming out to sea,
    believe the hyphenated tip-tear pages
marked and cut numerically.
    Would noble moles dig burrowed patches
leading democratic angles?
                                                  If not,
    consider then bulletproof roofs
with flags adjacent golden tiers.
    At once inside a mine for you
as best I could, candle-less,
    with fearsome beagles snapping
instamatics.
    Devoting each morning to relieving
centuries of dust caked carelessness
    all the while wile whales blew
through silent traffic.
    This pattern you've imprinted comes
along a longer line of impressions,
    and disturbance won't obliterate
this older sense of faith.

        Hapless and helpless I leave it to you.
        Calm and collected you leave it alone.

Tiny Town

She spent it all on no-vo-caine to keep those
        dreadful sparrows
from nesting on her stoop.
With an elevated high rise to guide her vision
        towards westward expansion
she sat on an inactive trip.
Dropping solicitations on updated ferries
        carrying conversational
table books kept me in time.
Pine away, dead soldier, and march
        to war in
Tiny Town Caskets.
Pass over tipsy stun guns tied to the hips
        of straight shooters
buzzing on to off the signs.
Of a finalized foundation of culture
        laugh at the
immobile structures that offer only shade.
And historical baggage sympathize with
        veterans of foreign wars
all pissed through indifference.

But if you ask me what's new,
don't.
Those who don't know me know best.
Bury the head in dynamite.
See what comes up.

Island Striped Hearts

With a sailor on your shoulder spitting
    fire, I drink alone.
There's a poster selling schedules
    along the avenue.
I collect another nickel on the dime
    where I belong.
Fighting faces in the hustle bustle cock
    block, pushing out.
Drop a dollar in the kitty with a bowtie on his neck.
Leave the stitches on the bitches burning out to the dawn.
Sulking out into the night where you could feel some self respect.
Touch a finger to her lips and you can tell it won't be long.

Bury bones along the river in a sing-song sassafras.
Leased bowbowbow Lupin couldn't push ahead.
Coming home to open arms and island striped hearts.
Button lock and zipped up combat.
Delegations to the last.

Seagull

Here   comes a
Cheer   for the
meaningless   words;
contemptible   contemplative words.
Those   gussied up
suits in rhetorical
jazz. Emphasizing emphysema.

I hope they find me loaded.
Singing in my baritone deaf man's howl.
Going on about the water and Lisbon,
in that self-inflated/self-important light from on the news.
With any luck, come plug me up
and send me to the gulls.
Give them some me do chew on.
Just not the don't have them talk.

This was when she had his dance.
I could try (had) but not tonight.
She told me to screw.
Had a drink on me.

Prospects & Veins

Consider this:
Progressive,
flexible,
a little more,
and listening.

This interest waxes out,
branched in subtly necessary trees,
and cornerstone memories of sensational foundations.
Conduct said jerking motion,
matching the tremors,
and slivers of cold.
Behave in dinner jackets,
and cut around a skirting business,
to reconstruct the martyr.

For this,
we maintain,
to think of a few scattered moments,
when time was much
smoother,
and the water was warm.

Rubber Mallet Stew

The claptrap filtered diamonds,
out a rubber mallet stew,
sucking strangers waiting for a bus,
on Sunday afternoon.

Recall the ammunition drills,
an accuracy in time,
ignoring stray hairs on your face,
watch you speak of California.

The bump to make a broken bed,
all tired sleep refused,
repeating old (you) songs new to me,
come to ruin in the fog.

Copper done knock the sensible,
stacked so neatly piled,
high,
avoiding public diuretics,
so we kiss as chemicals.
Love—s tooday?
No.
Bare convenience, at best,
honest purely as a fault.
Love—s ttoommoorrooww?
Maybe be.
I'll try to meet you there.

You Are the Book

Wrapping newsprint round,
         round, round
glass doll parts and
     severed children.
Placing filler in the
       Boxes, store them,
   stock them,
        warm & dry. Leave
me to my work. Discretely
       kiss my fingertips,
   at quarter past. Please,
      if you must,
bring butter knives around,
     around, around
to measure tombs each morning
        (the distance of fortune).
Keep warm, my
     Darling.
        Fake triumphant
     fire bombs, true enough
   for favors, low and dirty
double crosser.
        Think of me no
     more than usual, that
   is to say, not never.
And I will continue to drink my coffee.

Pickled

When that clean dusk settles
on my window in the cold,
the theories of demented pleasure
wear out my pickled eyes.
Loose springs go bumping out of habit
and in time they softly break,
with whiskey burps and snickers
I will dance across the coals.
Be it forward or malicious
we will swing a mighty blow,
to the single patient marker
bleeding out prophetic tongues.
Though some borrowed condensers
from a very honest friend,
we can hum as cats do
inside a jumping screen.
But until you cease said pleasure
if just to recognize,
how you started in steam
cannot speak your name.
So we slither & shout
to mark the way,
of where we haven't gone
and where we'd never be.

Peaches & Carrots

They brought the fields to her,
as she left us all in passing,
fully aware and incredibly simple,
we marched that old song.
A mumble fumble hand gesture,
like grabbing too tightly,
embarrassing,
shifting peaches & carrots,
to a brief clarity,
where the water can leap,
and wet kisses on your palm,
as I count your broken teeth,
and mild bandages.
But they brought the fields to her,
so softly by the road,
collaborative and numb.
Because I've seen you once before,
with veiled acceptance to show,
how quickly you can move,
around spaces filled up,
and in,
With peaches
&
Carrots.

Red Eagles All Loose

Can rascals go to heaven?
            Once there,
can they get in?

I've gotten so many nights,
            having no company,
        or too much.
What measures the proper amount?
Is there a proper amount?

Each model re-modeled, or spoken
            with laughter hopping down trickles,
        jokes in bed.

Those buggers all in,
            Red Eagles All Loose,
        while leaving me none the wiser,
to those pinch penny plots,
        that consume the daily motion.

OH! Leave me to pieces,
            and console your own skin!
        Guide no one to your windshield therapies.
Allow for grand mistakes of gratitude.

If not for your whole mess,
lest we dine on swine and leeks,
provide collection to the hull,
with captains pushing lilies.

                And let the rascals in!

I Sing For You

It has been too long
since I've watched you grow
& though these numbers
collected
can account for time lost
I sing for you.
Joyous accumulation
and misery mounts
& I sing for you.
Through Hell's summation
laughter and business
too many bold motions
I sing for you.
We bite the power lust
too few to count
& all those soggy nights
I sing for you.
Through troughs & gold
happy times
low tides and chum
I sing for you
Mice call out to arms & noise
With muted squeals under radiant poison
Briefcases of medicinal bricks
While I sing for you.
Your violence demands a ceasefire
I'm too busy to hear you
Because as your voice is mighty
I sing for you.

Bones of Spain

We spoke lengths of modern times
and old addresses
mostly,
but we had never touched upon
the unforgotten
evening.
Could shame police the progress low
and conversation
dwindle?
Without the bones of holy Spain
My Spanish is
horrendous.
We're laughing now and smack smack
hand to head a
fellow,
Your black eyes and wet nose
you must have ears.
Goat?
We're laughing now as good friends
as we amplify the
chances
that we will not sleep tonight
nor after that not
never.
But that is love as love
conveniently slow in its
rush.
I'll get the light and water
we will not
sleep.

Push & Pull
Me   Me

Their room sprawled out
     towards nautical ventures push
& pulled the curled you.
     Like salivating cash machines
suggesting proper station.
     Those days outnumbered future plans
leaving nostalgic vapors
     leaving weighted balloons.
Ideas of a memory to break your motivations
     and keep you underground.
The fear of realization
     could defeat all novices
arguing false derailment
     at the expense of superstition.
Someone was breathing her in.
     Watching recycled bitbitbit.
Follow all roads to the challenge
     from faded tattoos
and cheapo liquor.
     That all boils, to a point,
where no amount of purging
     can do a damn thing.
Gonna go onna walkabout.
     Waltzing Matilda.

Bosco!
No tongue!

Culture Shock

Feeling these as single strokes,
    in arrogance fond of dreaming,
Forced between pre-conceived notions
    & political preference.
If so,
    when down,
allow possible retraction,
    of personal ethos,
to play on glass balconies.
    Why the puffed up wigs?
Can simple children grow into these buttons?
    Grown into opinion through culture shock,
& genealogy,
    I have to laugh at you.
I'm much too scared to take you serious.
    Once I start,
the terror feeds inward.
    Go away to your social clubs.
I do not pray to owls.

Clean Faces

She was all as children were,
without the grace or style,
of wild flowers plucked and pruned,
she was all as children.
Unwashed
&
willing.
AND!
!OH!
How she willed it!

This professional operation,
connected as mesh humidity,
to be placed on sidewalk trees.
Invading foreign homes,
unfinished,
holy much as anything else,
in detecting rabies.
Roll without me, noble bone,
a dig, up your fortunate creation.

If we can ever stand apart again,
to brush our faces clean,
consider original work,
compared to recycled trash.

Politics

If
Any
Moreofthese
Stiff shirtclean
Motherfuckers
Ask me about my
Political stance one more
Time, I am going to grab them by
Their ears (iftheyhaveany) and
Throw them over the
Interstate.

Throwing a Fight

Sour buds & reach,
    these reasons can permit,
        dreaming, rolling, posthumous,
            with time held as an abstract.
A lock box filter,
    cold signing fit stigma,
        to stifle the restless officer,
            in love and outnumbered.
Polling, sideswipe,
    direct or discreetly,
        thinning up for orders,
            of timidity in diluted nature.
Waving tips of green,
    as old mourners tip over,
        throwing a righteous fight,
            in exchange for bereavement.

        Springing through skeletal ice.
        Low, behold my sentence.
        Run your hands over me.
        And know my regions.

Fizz Pop

Fizz!Pop!Wham!Pow!
Punch
A
River
Out
My
Face.
Hot!Hot!Hot!Hot!
Call
A
Taxi
Cab
For
Me.
No!You!Stand!Here!
I
Can
Make
It
Home
Myself.
HAH!HAH!HAH!HAH!
Tell
Your
Wife
I
Said,
"Hello."

Oh!No!You!Don't!
Put
Your
Money
In
The
Door.
Fizz!Pop!Wham!Pow!
Punch
A
River
Out
My
Face.

Adventures in Theft

When time and location call for great decisions,
    reason can be sacrificed.
Replaced, then, without warning, or reason,
    delicious dangers pollute pallets.
You can never eat caution again, different,
    canned quietly by blander hands.
Oh, sure, they said there was their own,
    bitter old bastard down south.
You took the trip from curiosity,
    pleased to treat nobody right
And as seasonal regiment pomp,
    I knew it had come to this.
So allow most of history a pardon,
    and please tend to my home.
I will be leaving to find work,
    shucking clams in an emerald.

Drweam

I've t
    a
    k
    e
    n
    consideration, Specific
DANGER! & consequence, from int0 yer
        Black Spring.
    This motivation ekes
               along towards sinister outcomes
colorized(finitely)by cowardice.
              Patiently,
      Dignified |-------------------------------| Politely
           drweam.
        Homespun Collections
         of filthy habits
         to help us

                                sleep.

But we don't receive any.

        Signal outside sources,
cold cold cold &small.
With a modest sensation of self worth,
    allow me to depart.

           Patiently
      Dignified |-------------------------------| Politely

         And
          Never
        Let
         Me
       Stop.

Comes in Bunches

If I could
    my darling dear
one in a one in a one   please
keep me behind eyes   please
your secret technique   please
of hostage temptation   please
collect me   please
as I had sought your face   please
& hands   please
to wash each other   please
in acrobatic torments   please
believe each my very lie   please
as I have yours   please
this quiet request   please
can only convenience   please
the free time   please
reveal your terrors   please
in trusting me   please
or cursing me   please
as I do curse you   please
implicitly   please
as all hate stems   please
from reflects of love   please
know this   please.

The Fink

AfixquickfixA
rounded out to you, the math.
How can you be so bold?
A liberation vines of ivy
on one dollar brick buildings
across the river.
The face,
covered,
with symmetric curves
that stand in isolation
be tightened them out with the cold.
Your ears,
blocked,
with supersonic reducers
have lessened their potential touch.
Your hands,
cracked,
in solid pain situations
can scramble inout.

AquickfixquickA
sectioned around me, the fink.
Where do the limits meet?
Distractions in light construction
meant for a big planner
in a tuxedo.

Find Me

I have seen Mars; the impossible friend
winking like a stranger
across a crowded reef.
If the numbers part out
to clear a heading, that's grand,
then you may find me there.
I have found a cave, the hidey-hole
sounding as a kettle drum
thrown deep the well.
Gather the torches
and dynamite, dry,
to blast me out.
I know a hollow tree, very soft
and amicable
though the smell is damp.
Bring axes, well sharpened,
but do come alone
I have a surprise.
If I do come over, wherever you are
wearing old skin
a bit rough,
I will wave my hands
to that your face.
The foundation to my home.

. . . .

Dreamscapes

Living through it, you were there.
A soul survivor in fortuitous grips.
Recalling portions from dreamscapes,
and the mutants found therein.
Certain phrasing, specifically,
moves as your likeness
to collect loose tears
on a bowery stoop.
Some foulmouthed divers,
munching deep to sea,
dig up pearls for musky women
all smoking drunk.
I love it.

Should misfortune guide you
or walk beside your stumble
then ascend sure noble legs
where you can build your city

When searching for the great pulse,
a bag of new faces and names,
be sure to request certain phrasing
in order to know avoidance
of the loose bowery tears.

Somewhere in the Dirt

So now time was spent
marking all indiscretions not
as benefit but as pull
to leave this place course.
Somewhere in the dirt
where nothing can grow
but all is but buried down deep
you may find some honest job.
For the love left unchallenged
but blinded as right
or unwavering kindness
will only fill a pocket.
Bring 'round a skin
tight as they come
for refusal diesel oil
to water me down.
Blow out all fear
big as a house
and you will see yourself
in harm's blessed way.

At the Whitney House

This stumbler
        wasted
in a thick brogue & with tiny earnings
     witnessed obscenity
at the Whitney House.

However road apples can find
     the thrilling tumble and push
shooting sonic insulation
     as my heart fills with bourbon
at the Whitney House.

Some beautiful mites hold
     on some dusty old souls
or they're painting the cellar
     with bright orange
at the Whitney House.

There's a lady librarian
     with a tattooed love
and an old box of records
     they'll sell you some wax
at the Whitney House.

And people can live there
     if you don't mind the noise
please join me tonight
     I have some good friends
at the Whitney House.

And That's That

There was talk of a man
living outside of Jackson
served thirteen long years
out a hole from a pistol
with a family sedan
and some words from a farmer
I suspect they will burn him
there next to his father.

I knew a woman
who dancing on tables
would quote E. E. Cummings
and kiss like a monster
they found her there crying
"They're coming to kill me."
she left when I mentioned
that I may still love her.

Now time is a child
with sixteen long fingers
for which it divies
the potential for knowledge
for dynasties holding
a shiny new power
go waste it away &
just skip all the rough stuff.

The theories abound
to inform us of answers
and coddle the suckers
who can't get to sleep
while burglars charge interest
and rapists write speeches
please don't kiss my baby
I'll knock out your teeth.

A Solid
personality.

Panic Eating

And then she eats my book,
                panic eating.
We started on foot
                swaying out
with 6,000 watches.

I hope to end near
                a fumble kind of
falling down.
                Roll with it.
            Know your ground.

All enemies are capable
                but only some are willing.
From a Gregorian target
                transposed
from a collapsible tone
            intended for children
over 8 years old.

Press 1

For a brief and complicated answer,
press 1.
To know who will love you unconditionally,
press 2.
For the universal explanation,
press 3.
To receive unlimited power,
press 4.
To speak to an operator,
press 5.

Snubby

The untapped pleasure from a miserable day,
        and here I am cursing Plato,
and trying to work,
        or do nothing.
Nothing sounds good.

But everything is appealing.
        and these, the phobic plots,
simple as they stand,
        generating these sensations;
there can be peace at the bottom,
        near the collected river.

Come take out my body,
        move me all over the day,
but excuse my stutter,
        and sleepy smile.

I've only been here a short while,
        you see?
Hah, hah, hah!
        What snubby items we steal!
Pass me over the water,
        and let me cool my jets.

Science

now,
if you lift this part
here,
we can see into the cellar.
but,
when you push this in
there,
you can see me naked.
and,
if you'd like to,
really,
I would appreciate it.

Just
Roses.

Whiskey & Beans

No Retreat @ 3 AM

A gentle three-day rain.
        Warm enough for walking
too cold to swim.
        She'll be springtime fancy
& I can barely stand up.
        So when you let me collect
abbreviations,
        pets & relics,
whiskey & beans,
        or a new mattress,
we can have each all night
        and feel no serious debt.

Maybe though we plan
        five or ten to fifteen
circumstances waltzing at chaos
        to muck up the works.
So screw it.
        We can fix it in editing.
While we cut ourselves up
        and dig deeper than before.

Scarce

Dumb no more.
Not in silent dreams.
Rampaging houses both
old and familiar
with quiet children
that stay indoors.
Build my fancied structure
of anxious puddle jumpers
to carry what little we have
to those who need it less.
Tell me a story.
Make me break down
as like the stranger feast
when the animals low
and all peoples know better.
I sit as one can sit well
begging posture to be
natural.
Come live with my house.
Familiarize completely
my loose boards
old paint, brass beds
and animals.
I will try to be scarce.

Who Can Say?

Can you tell me how
why, where, and with whom
you have settled your divine nest?
I have tried several times
(several)
to somehow manifest.
Observations, however,
Lead me up stray catwalks of night bleach,
mornings of unsuitable horrors,
and boiling water beds.

If for whatever reason
you should think me kind or possible
take note from where I've left off
and process your assumptions.
Believe no promise of luck
to project coincidental happenstance.
The work involving honest sweat
bold odors from men in the sun
with tired eyes that hurt
straining to see.
Will laborious time be found abroad?
A pension or wages to settle these waves?
Shall fortune sink upon slumped shoulders
as fat pigeons filled with happiness?
Who can say?

The News

The potential paper brigade
have drowned the macrobiotics.
No style of wit or deception push push
the clarity of your words.
Set each of your steps as a trap you can see
but stumble blind and smiling.
Go rigmarole into piles of moisture
while sucking time titties around.
Collar the children you knew as a youth
they're out there wandering in.
Tighten a finger to follow the fist
and spell your mighty name.
Listen around her subliminal needs
her porous sense of pride.
Mysterious colors presented as such
will fashion a singular guide.
The news will come
just as the night
so wait until
the break.

All Over Town

There's a bright old man
in a great big hole
and he laughs with a very little dog.
He can roll big words
when his mouth is tight
and he never calls your name
all over town.

She's a big city slip
with a foreign laced tongue
doing what she likes to do all day.
These tobacco riddled kids
bounce all over her knees
and you'll see her working nights
all over town.

In a meat house plant
on assembled lines
stands a student of a selfless name.
He can sing about a girl
play piano, drink a beer
and he walks along the night
all over town.

There's a big green house
off a sideways street
where I left a little happiness behind.
Not a chance to get it back
or even borrow it a day
and you'll find my empty steps
all over town.

The Sum of 2

Suspected ailments collect
inside of your wormy protein
all by telephone.
"No, its fine."
"Yes, I'm better."
Liar.
Directed as most to measure derailment
for pockets of crumpled bills.
The chase of one-thousand
sinners; cascading with vast polarities.
Cheap.
Some floating off adrift
towards all necessary statements
milling about.
A thought quota.
Daily disappointments.
Child.
Temper, temper
little devil collector
sitting on a cliff.
Isolated.
Bothered.
Familiar.

Bilge Pump

false conversations with puffery

Magnificent bilge
forcing great exits
down new areas
to contaminate no one.
I'd rather pull out
my own teeth
than smell those terrible
tubes.
No good for picnics
or games
but decent fishing
and fabulous prizes.

Ask about their.
Or take a loot at.
Just don't try the.
And please watch your.

Settled as good as law
mixed sarcastic deficant.
So long as you remain
I will not be instigating
the stuffed conversation.
I'll be down the ravine
in search of more bones.

Twiddled & Fiddled

A sneer to you

No party girls have
like big peacock blow
outstanding starts
Twiddled & Fiddled
from a sticky backseat
to imported lettuce.

Porcelain umbrellas
misguided handbags
all portions exaggerate
bigger concepts
inclusive packages
credit cards

When those options come standard
requested by boasters
enacting relief and slouch
smaller than the deals
of guaranteed
social jaundice.

Hallelujah Jones!
Killed by comfort.
Question:
Have you have what we need?
Verily?
Unthinkable!

A Grand Number

Shall we be to whom structure shows?
All bent half way from knees to nose?
Then measure some static filtration tonight,
and stick your indignation.

Can we be they that hold handsome questions?
Lying on side ways to aid in digestion?
We'll have to correct the position at hand,
I cannot see the screen.

Direction from crooked blood thinners dreaming?
Allowing persuasions of vanity scheming?
Pleasantly growing to a grand number,
a ruse at first glance.

Would you admit your open hope?
That small begging sound wrapped all up in a rope?
I know for a fact it can dangle,
like loose skin on a pinch.

The Meal

Portioned out to great amounts
spread on bulk and quarry
left as altered moderation
offered of a helping hand.
Breaching upwards angles darting
in a round-about motion
playful as every memory
to be adjusted accordingly.
Apologetic and free of regret
simple geometry in action
measured with grievances
of a splintered friendship.
These are the recipes
as for the meal incomplete
years of preparation cornered
by an inconvenient time.
Eat it slowlydrink it inbut save some roomthere will be more.

In Bed

In times when you share a bed
there is a lot to consider.
Will she be kind in the morning fog?
Will I?
Does she drool and speak softly
of other boys she knew?
Will there be fits of spastic laughter?
I have been known to do this.
There will be:
cover coveting
sheet keeping
pillow snatching
and the occasional
kick.
I will wish to sleep alone
under these demands
Until I do.
Then I sleep a little sadder
than before.
Let us push a new bill of shared insomnia.
Alert
frisky
chatty
drinking
exhaust all nocturnal activity
and permit sleep to wash over us both.
Welcomed
apathetic
day-light
free time.
As I sleep upon my hand
wake me in the afternoon
so we may greet the night.

The Mild

And direction assumes point
so perspective is a myth.
Gather, instead, wavelength
outstretched in weeping sonar.
Responsive as collected as composure can be
as radical o those who swear by it.
But if you should be shaken
terrified or drunk
hopefully both
go until broke bottom to core.
The mild can only learn from wonderful mistakes.
Danger builds an appetite
food tastes better post-fear
and you must try the wine.
So call out some strangers or
if you can manage
a tiger.
No one will bother you
if you have a tiger.

The Night of the Three-Hour Fire

When we had to play music for money

On the night of the three hour fire
    dance demons flipped a pleasure stroke
the top of my head came off
    and she pushed pussy arrows all around.
Like vaginal Indians on a wagon train.
    We swam as confused seamen
digging sweet and low-down
    trying to press our hands
around time knives and butter.

Loose status paraded tattoos
    advertising the British invasion
requesting slower motions
    or just a night or two.
Captain Parrot shined a light
    Indulging three dumb sticks
to offer a small pittance
    for the folly of a fib.

As the confidence altered sound
    and gravity lead to noise
and more hands spread skyward
    and temperatures rose
and you lost your teeth
    and I shook
the night of the three hour fire
    lost me.

The Rate at Which I Fall in Love is Unhealthy

Spreading down sounds
    on wetness out of season
pressing each finger together
    as comfortable security.
Specter bless my sight
    in passing fancy
or immaterial solution
    of reality phasing.
Dually roll-a-roll-a
    tossing rocks and milk and honey
pierced a muscle in a fracture
    yelling out of your mind.
Kicking names on dirty floors
    with a confident nod to the dead
Whose exhausted efforts collect
    impairing the active response.

Vagrant of Meager Impositions

Spontaneity drives me home
    to impulsive lover's dream
aptly sampled in collision
    with adjoining corner space.

Partnered up as he will know
    what then who should slowly start
or to where our training leads
    and by when should we arrive

Vagrant of meager impositions
    pusher, jumper, cornerstone
the pipipipi direction
    run back as a name.

Alterations to:
    1.ceasefire
    2.bepolite
    3.flake
    4.embitter

Glowing among violet winds
    stir my guts.

Behavioral Noise

Language
(asaprison)
holding personal insight
blocks you.
Selective ammunition
(forspecificcalibration)
must be misunderstood
joyfully.
Isolation will be
(asiunderstandit)
a song to guide blind missions
past manic calculations
and repetitious behavioral noise.
False memories
(andopenagendas)
blow it up to bug out
keep that beaten phrasing
like no one has before.
But you knowknowknownono.

Obelisks and Monoliths

Braced onto concrete and brick
may you stand as low interrogations;
education transmitted by thugs
obelisks and monoliths,
sights left peeling outward
and away from most misery.
Should you, are to find
be brimming set to boil
feelknow my quiet hands
in a fondness for figure
in memory maps.

You courageous bastard!
How come you shave so close?

You to which sugar melts
from a gesture of kindness.
Kept as that frozen feature
so you be bored dumb
looking through everything
from the distance of 7 miles.
Creased as marked fold
a referral note
not being noteworthy
in a broken colossus.

Reminders

Returning to the front,
once considered as the back,
speculating the when to where
of which you will break.
Flash bombs and tracer bullets
those tired old roads
piles of greasy cash
all memory/no news.
In the event of repeat offenses
downing capsulated doom
register solar awareness
plan plan darker days.
Upon smoky recollection
immaculate loss
or beastly advances
laugh at yourself.
Get planned through & through
predictable as reliable signs
almost quite dull
reminders.
Feel out a dangerous kit
building nano-mechanisms
collected from soiled wigs
all painted to turn.
Pray for forever to ever return
so to wait by a cosmic reducer
completing countdowns of chance
while maintaining faith in chaotic whim.

Something Me Birds

When the last of my tolerance
        for rhythm & motion
reaches it's peak
        you can find me during sleep
                        something me birds.

Groups of 3-4 gangsters
        hiding in memories bookstore
thumbing through recipes
        & romance
                        something me birds.

Sharing bland rolls executive
        ones that peel away
during measurements
        of cigarette rations
                        something me birds.

A self conscious exhibitionist
        waiving his wares throughout
asking you not to stare
        begging you to
                        something me birds.

One to hurt your enemies
        or your friends
one to share some truth
        it was called
                        something me birds.

Who's Who

Stubborn & direct when isolated.
Quiet & passive in groups.
Brave & daring in theory.
Shrinking & jumpy in practice.
In massive volumes of pure dialogue
with nothing wasted or neglected
a surprise come out today.
The who's who made a what what
enough to build four homes
or chanting houses.
Come get literal indoors
along tattered rags of longing.
For what, specifically, diverts
most energy into momentum?
A common goal found in absence
or the desire for understatement.
Call off grey stragglers that make up your mind.
Incinerate fond ideals thought to speak.
Pierce large holes into your name.
Smother the pillars of design.

The Sudden Season

As they sing again in code,
                    mixing all sorts of trouble
in ritualistic courtship
                    for the sudden season,
rising out of dirty water dripping,
                    she fixes her hair.
He'll fake an illness of grandeur,
                    shaking head and hands opposing
leaving vague descriptions impartial
                    to relocate among the weeds,
hoping he may have an angle
                    as the anxious occupier.

This being their final evening
arrangements have been made
insurance for a primal display
guaranteeing completion.

ᚖᚖᚖ

L.S. enters the dream

Voluminous lengths & care to detail
in pleasure knowing & sudden.
Abroad leading bitters & sour mash flow
controlling the rolling & speed.
The number of guests & cause of the start
decides on my patience & courage.

I was lead through the you
and into the larger you
counted fair and debutant with
pink & green dogs.
No nonsense
just pink and green dogs.

Scholastic entanglement presented opinions,
citing quotes & sources blindly smile,
though through aesthetic spectacular
broad, bold, confident
those demanded who for change.

Blood chips on the carpet &
the smell metal.
Crisp introspection on ethnic traditions,
the spread that made Solomon weep,
& 4 goddamn hours of starvation.
As you would feed one sand.

eateateat
&&&

White Noise

A set of repeater dolls, as advertised,
     coupled with two stiffs, respectively,
     were talking about their jobs.
My crew washed tonsils as professionals,
     hard at work to manage accounts,
     to see who would be stiff.

Room buzz was a vacuum for noise,
     chatter noise, white noise
     speculation, disagreement,
     pleasure centers held attention.
Before the muscle arrived,
     before the Baghdad battery,
     before swollen intentions,
     we danced a lot of time.

     Spinning as repeater dolls, as advertised,
       with nothing close to grace.
     I left as the deviated location sank further
     to options of smoke cellars of burlesque.

     Her name was Ginger, but I doubt it.

Buy a Little Basket

Sadly & Otherwise

People will often dramatize
or fondle
that great big love.
But this reality
or unsure fantasy
to those who have lived it
is flexible.
Gather up your needs
neurosis & phobias
and buy a little basket
so the weight distribution,
balanced,
does not trip you up.
Be aware that some
songs know no love
though they sing
sadly & otherwise.

Write your own damn song
and be happy
that you can write at all.

Pressure Waltz

Among extensive smells with strange new tones,
what people can move so?

These bellows call for action from the drip,
with some hope for stillness there.

A slight drop force swept in plague fields,
not especially for benefit.

Judging pint flames of choice plumes,
geometric giants shot panic.

Tumultuous in force through fear
a powerful condemnation of will
and love as interrogation
washed up the beaches we knew.

NecessaryNecessaryNecessary
to call out locations for deconstruction
or general dismantling.

Watching the procession
of time & space spread
through oiled boards
mu tongue froze up
my reason.

{ ///// ✕ \\\\ }

DROW
NING
ASRA
TSCA
NINA
BARR
ELOF
SPIT
ANDP
ISSC
ANDE
STRO
YSOM
EOFT
HEHA
PPIE
RMOM
ENTS
OFWH
ATCO
ULDH
AVEB
EEN.

Ramadactyls in a Bozo Dream

Pistol pod jumping from a fresh cat nightmare
Jeep tuck roll shout call my name
Falling on a floor beneath a sailor's station
Next exit prove the new toilet frenzy.
Laugh a louder notion than you had expected
Dresses a messes up break you nose
Feeling up a girl that shows a slight brain damage
Spending all the money you had made last week.
Polyester jack-boots clipping the tulips
Meager eager beavers hanging on for life
Stopping on a dropper in a station wagon
Eyes are rolling back along the Tappan Zee.
Chest pump thumping on a naughty notion
New ramadactyls in a bozo dream
Sucking on your tongue among a dry spell season
Save it for the humble rumble barley sack.

I'll
Take
It.

Silhouettes of Singapore

Silhouettes of Singapore
wedged inside the future of maybe
either swallows or bats
transportation.

Tearing up a filibuster
holding palm flat out front ways
slowing to a stop
maintenance.

Passion found me
hiding in a waste bucket insolent
kicking and screaming
smiling.

Wasting ignorance up
as divided distribution
retreating a failure
pro.

Then that dignified & weathered look
Oh, glorified in song & film
quietly fell all around me
inviting a fluent indifference.
Now Sham 69,
or the Stiff Little Fingers?
I don't know where they've gone.

Observe Radio Silence

Oh please shut up.
And stuff it, hush, and shhh.
No more, no more.
I'm done for, please.
Let me tell you now,
before you start again,
stop talking.
Your sleep patterns bore me.
You have no sex life, and I'm sorry.
I know it's funny, just laugh.
I hate that song.
I don't like your dog.
All unhappy jobs are shit.
Yes, she likes you.
Not right now.
Ask him later.
Shush.
Keep the fucking change.
Just let me scribble and smoke.

Dirty Stinger

Contact!
Push with;
Stinger.

Dirty in nature, otherwise clean
clean is safe, safe is dull
strike the cleaners down!

Orange peels on a luxury trip
keep talk 'bout nothing
at great lengths.

Queen de-fanged.
Whatever potential was,
not nothing no more.

Empty shells wrap arms about
giving a block head
and some reach-a-roos.

Where do I sign up?
Is there training for this neglect?
. . . doubtful.

Maybe find some time to leave.

But Then We Are Again

Boxed loosely stow,
        a rising scale of discharge,
singing out from your brisket,
        some dirty old song.

Paw this leadership down,
        etching cerf-volant departments
violin solos,
        & group efforts.

Commanding illustrated fog,
        but then we are again,
leaning forward and bright,
        bellowing optimism.

Patting catatonic rituals,
        Infinite loans of measure,
stalking plans of promise,
        stolen in the night.

Drive on & pull the force,
        filing dimensional rabbits,
in the name of a madman . . .
        what was his name?
        Her name?
        Their name?
        nuts.

Regardless, we press on tomorrow to know where we were,
but then we are again.

Laughter You See

Flavors in domino allowance
outlines for free
a showman undefined
waters it down.
Pinks in the summer loft
blues in the noon
clammy hands fumble pockets
lighting a match.
Eyes on the makeshift
cream on the rim
jabbing a questionnaire
in the throat.
Some stylized waitress
crying on break
hiding a rubber hose
in her purse.
Human sweat & pheromones
laughter you see
appearing there nightly
by request.
Ocular misdirection
fire or foe
dragging me by the ears
to a room.

In the Din of Attempt

In the din of attempt
throw everything else away.
Keep sporadic time
jumping as you sleep.
Rest on fire like lovers who do;
their do can fix most anything.
Be such the rogue
to whomever sits still
firmly grounded in stagnant water.
Immediate altercations require
vague reasoning
and small favors to compensate/
for a lack of compensation.
Cut out,
immigrant,
pilgrim,
paper doll who smooth
walking in the din of attempt
can fold under pressurized lids
smoking cold in the blue.
I will leave you like
I found you dusty
cramped & poor
muscled out
of here
right
now.

Custom Suit

Free to collect scraps
Sorry to eat out
Quick to be quiet
Eager to clean
Willing to blow jokes
Bitter with mercy
Graciously appalling
Cheap in bed
Dirty in the shower
Cozy as misdirection
Noble when cheating
Completely insane
Ugly when shopping
Dumb as a lump
Fearful of you
Stubborn in church
Bored with luck
Long in the tooth
Tired of money
Obsessed with time
Fond of eating
Loves to fight
Nervous on the line
Calm on fire
Difficult to reach
Drawn & quartered
Spontaneously dry
Non-responsive
Filled with junk
Slow to apologize

& Teasing

Undress come easy amateur
bit lip all look uncertain
practice mirror figure
try a little bit.

Grooming
       Looming
             Unassuming
Small to quick & teasing.
Wrap me
all in your fever
to settle neatly
in heat.

Oh yes, I am an amateur
cocksure in solid doubt
loudly shaking storms
just to be heard.

As proof of guarded leaning
staring indirect or pierced
match my elasticity
synchronize our pulse.

Liquored
up &
Naked

Trolley Rosters Minced a Timetable

Like another speed trap
RICKETY-AT-AT-AT-AT
Catch these turns often
in re-re-reanimated dimension.
You break down the line
into three more stooges
a rubber Pygmalion
to send your note.
Trolley rosters minced a timetable
sleeping at 6:00 AM
listening to garbage trucks
while answering doors.
Aspiring finsters replicate
a clicking wheezing tick
to say,,,,,
      "I'm working, watch me listen."
      But it's too damn hot to try.
Pinch me,
      I'm there,
Oh,
      My,
            Please,
Yes,
      Yes,
Call a doctor friend
      You know,
The surgeon on
      The pink.

A Dry Simpleton

Draft to lean a dry simpleton
smirky for concealment blush
OhIknowyouknowheknew
'cause it happened once before
when the big one came.
We scraped out each morning
holding the rails for life
not as dearly as demonstrated
watching old army science
reviving dog parts.
Shuffling through all the best
& worst invented prize
caring too much
but neglected enough
till the next time.
Barging these glimpses
out and over fog bay,
advertising dancing girls
with men too young to die.
I'll leave you to yourselves
playing sticky cake roulette
let me through leg or tether.
On belay?
Belay on.

My Voice; A Terror

Surface warfare
 expanding on loose boards
each and every one affected.
 New friends at breakfast
at that unreachable point
 All seem longer than the norm.
Shaggy noise outsmarts a tube
 and I've just received word
on a flying car.
 Tremors rip through me
my voice; a terror
 choking off and on.

Women keep track of these things.

They have told me more
 than once
about what time is
 and to spend it with whom.
All I have is time
 but more is good.
More to make
 or crumble
  in patience
   and modesty
  combinations
  leap frog
 in riverbanks
and yacht swamps.

-(4)-

Hefty coincidences
dripping all nowhere
and so you don't got no more?
Not like the neighbors fit
as liars.
Honest in—(4)-
Faith in—(4)-
reasonless antiques
will never understand perfection
when everything ends.
Except—(4)-
which will
have to always be.
Keep the rest,
all of it please,
but leave me—(4)-
to discuss the plans
& universal calamity.
Pull down your beat.
Leave it here.

Melancholy Zen

March of the wooden Koan
swaggering lily white preference
Whistling a tune of morphic resonance
wondering out loud.
Goose legged valley gap
as the true soldiers tell
of conquests & invasions
deployment or retreat.
Allow collation the precious
impudent second hand
inching on and on to it
with painful ascension.
Cutting bush of refuse bins
standing at attention
along a veteran's shelter
foiled again.
Stones of centuries' weight
carry inconsistencies.
In the right kind of light
it's infuriating.

Avenues of Permanence

Poster child picked up
      and rolled out of insolent creases
he opted for jitters.

Fixing his grease,
      some fabrications landed
down ways.

Out there now rolling-olling-olling
      kicking out plays
as though he had once.

Dark was the box
      he would rattle along
with him.

Two volcanoes were bubbling
      in daisy-duke pukes
completely in love.

So much so that his patterns
      almost accurately always
missed a cross-hatch Johnny.

Struck in and all over
      avenues of permanence
my goodness, no.

Relieve me of sedation
      in something like a drum
repeating your tired old self.

Wee Three Kings

We got wet all night
lit some fires on the couch
found a new hole
and slipped into unconsciousness.

Wee three who got scared
jumpy at the thought
chin up and gazing
towards Heaven and Pluto.

Can we fit in the tub?
Almost,
got it.

Just don't look at her
or her perfect body.
Jokes are safe and easier.
"Pass it over this way."

Dizzy readin's
Onner shrrt
"beer pussy weed"

Three Kings
Wholy Trinity
Aye Carumba!

Morning then grabbing dream clips out from a fish and into my schedule.
One more coffee/one more egg/goodbye my friends/I'm off to work.

Lipstick Spittoon

Dented again
tracked on back to back
to back
all teeth to ear
like you know.
Pain sucked into the sound
often heard by drinking glass
or negligee
fit for pigs.
Formed in fiction
surreal-ity manifest
spies & cages
dropped from a plane
into a field.
Not my favorite
or stunning attempt
jangled through tunnels
and a lack of oxygen
for you.
Hindered by a dialogue
the shining distraction
a lipstick spittoon
kicked in the side
dented again.

2,000 False Starts

She's all thick with language
older than the years weighed
in her blood.
Her name resonates from & through
passing tremors & shakes
waking my dead.
For now muffled & suppressed
I can cough quietly hiding
behind rounded minds.
2,000 false starts
mimic dipping cold water
speaking out twice
just to remember something.
Come back, Petunia
& listen to them.
Come back, Marcus
& surface relief.
Look as you feel.
Feel as you look.

He Looks Poor

Wrinkled in a flirt
all eyes & smile
quiet laugh
where language takes a turn.
Swaying all nighttime music
dripping down concrete gin
posted with emergency contacts
& cocaine.
Shy bashful for button lip
how dry I truly am!
Concentrating
know not what not to say.
whoop, she said it,
astride her horse faced
friend . . .
mean mugging from her get-go.
Leaving no chance for the wicked.
Larcenous with that face
nowhere near her friend
my friend.
For what friends deny glance stares?
Approaching the wonder
of curious beauty
I started to speak
before her horse had enough
and saddled her up.

"Don't talk to him,
he looks poor."

Christ, Jesus

Terrified of motorcycles,
        he collapsed twice.
So the sounds ripped out
        from under his legs
the carpet of reason.
Pleading for hot water pennies
        and shadow play smoke,
I comply.
To which he describes the devil
        and declares himself Christ, Jesus.
His hair is gone
teeth
eyes gone
        no ears, no shoes.
Just tongue sucking
        spit string
smacking hateful racism
        as I hold the door.

Don't let the bastard in!

The professional drunks
        in storybook suits
living as devoted enemies
        to the future grime
smacking his gums.

He pointed down the street
said something
& moved on down the line.

And Everything is Louder

How many shows today?
And which will be solid
in the aetherial moss of
big arms doubled over
their growing concern?
For when bliss encroaches
nights, before weighing
in heated portions,
drive a while low from
the start.

Reviewing scrambled lectures
handled delicately whereabouts
the center of a shelter
circumvents magnetic north.
Upon entry or diversion,
into or out by in-between;
like flash card pictures
on some private island,
remark out of vivid silk
veiling locomotion eternal
when you start to fall asleep
and everything is louder.

Slip your courage invisible.
Making your ends as
a rest,
in the hopes of completed
sleep,
so as not to wake up
tired,
or any more surprises.

Crowns Inside

Should it be told?
The dollhouse dinner with
failed apple endings?
The crooked hook pipe on
a smoking lawn?
The mind of meeting as
fingerprint skin?
How proudly laughter paraded up
& down the steps of candy stone
impression.
Proud and selfless as once aforementioned.
Selfless in a guided group pulse
spouting foreign Lou-Lous to
pinhole manners.
Show me what you like so far;
from what you've seen balance
in creative concern.
Maybe necessary as a king
of persistent images
ghosted along the outer wall
and starting down shine.
In less we've done worse.
Though time is none the wiser
we are here to when again.
Perhaps a maybe chance chance
simmering a stew.
Drive a spoon among the field.
Create the great spot
with crowns inside an opening
once closed so long ago.

Chalet Debris

I will no longer pretend to speak
        from dry spell well water
garnering life in a bucketed rope.
            I would please, if you please,
                rather touch upon the topic
            of where the sun hits you first
                so as to be all seen.
Do not approach my admiration
        as ready perversion.
The body of work
        you present in the autumn
undoubtedly clouds
        the previous season.
            Along the chalet debris of memory
                lazy drifting past faces
            & minor exaggerations
                I count impulses on one hand
            scrutinizing each passing finger.
Beginning again to when
        we awoke in our own
comfortable absence. Knowing
        all roads, we dig down, down past
the grass seed and rooted
        light which shifts as a
ticker bone.

Oh we'll toss meanwhile's
     past our by-the-ways and
further-mores.
     That being said, navigate well.
Move tubs of grain sand boxes
     trucked a moment in
motion staccato skipping
     the song of a pain filled
head woman; she's over on the left.

On Rambling

On rambling, I say, to
whose anchor you've set?
Not mine, you say, but
the chain link is heavy.
More news, if you could, of
new waves near the water.
But me, if I could, would
stop feeding the fish.
A pic-box, you see, has
assembled some time.
While thumbing, I see, thick
with gloss of the glaze.

        But what of we has novelty marked?
      Simple comedies under wigged mask handle.
      Dancing resistant to rheumatic shivers
        call work from pale hands that
        fearing nothing but amputation
          move incontrovertibly
          on obscene necks.

Conjuring up the pic-box
as seen across the world
of soiled linens & oil lamps
of canvas & stolen charm
the mind repeats a phrasing
long thought reversed & broke
but found to be asleep.

On rambling, you say, to
whose anchor you've set?
Not yours, I say, but
the chain link is heavy.

End to End

MARCH AND DOT THE DOGE!
Safely as commanders' shape.
Do not allow in curious times
a fascination commonplace.
Permit, instead, a dully head
all talk&spit&cry.
And eat to moan to burn too
brightly luminescent pander.
On harbor's disenchanted sea based
singularly unopposed
go stand a friend from
end to end
again to measure merit.
Just low enough as
low can be before some
kind of touching.
Some shiny stare down boogy-
woogy inching for undressing.
Let them out to smart conditions
sturdy in the dry.
Right above a younger rocket
grounded on a stick.
Liver leash among control
inserting intuition.
With borderlands of limit
rumored from depth
fishing Aphrodite
laughing on a hook.

My Witless Age

Ill thought, come back again.
Diminish, please, my witless age.
A sloppy tongue from foam
& color coddle as a rush.
Just how the longing so presumed
or common & expected
could focus all attentions like
a dirty joke review.
I think of better cartilage
and ladders to the roof
where all of night collapses
as an awful stone.
Withered among sweet air
patted onto caked faces
covering the natural scent
of an uncertain fear.
Spread them out in silver
tightly knit to a fault.
Outside my calculations
single double triple checked
friends report the worst of it
wearing my wear.
For now I wait for wisdom's sake;
and older, kinder me,
to snap and hiss or hum the ready
stranger older tune.

Thanks
For Stopping
By.
Don't be
a putz.

Acknowledgments

Some people have been dually responsible for this in one way or another. Either through direct involvement or by being a bunch of helpful sticks, you're just at fault :

—Nicholas Adams—Todd A. Davis—Daniel Gursky—Sean O'Neil—Allison McNamara—Zack Wilson—Narath Serei—Kelly McGuire—Jason Huggins—Alston Shackelford—Danielle Serafini—Gabrielle Ahern—Dimitri Karouta—Kendal Fox—Leah, Willie, and Izzy—Keith Dooley—Carmine Lavieri—Rachel Koelsch—Hannah Borkowski—

Made in the USA
Middletown, DE
05 December 2015